The Earthworm Jar

David Appelbaum

CODHILL PRESS

'The Earthworm Jar' and 'Returning to the Nest' first appeared in *Commonweal.* 'Herding Toward the Ark' first appeared in *The American Poetry Review.*

Library of Congress Cataloging-in-Publication Data

Appelbaum, David.
The earthworm jar: poems, 1993-96 / David Appelbaum.
p.cm.
ISBN 1-930337-01-9 (alk. paper)
I. Title
PS3551.P557 E28 2001
811'.54--dc21
00-060270

The Earthworm Jar

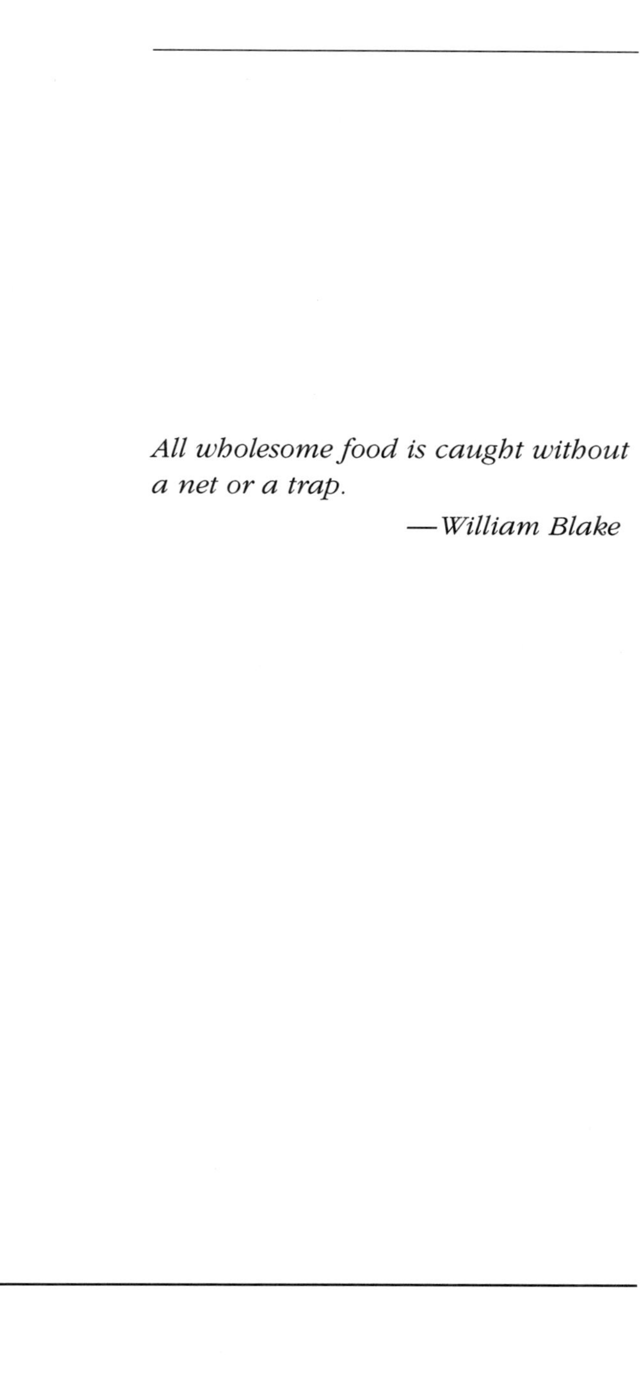

All wholesome food is caught without a net or a trap.

—William Blake

The Poems

The Earthworm Jar

In an Oval Glass

Herding toward the ark

White sheep in the trees
blown by heavy rains
white fleece in the belly of the hill.
All day I stir barley
in an iron pot by the stove
while rain drips in.

It is steady, hooves
on the bridge to the fold.
The bucket's full
but they keep on coming,
pearls dropping to the bottom,
white tails down to the bottom
of the sea.
I want to see the ewes lie
on the dry hay.

By night it is different.
The sheep have their barley breath
& don't want my eyes on them.
In the dark we are not the same.
They know I keep a gun.

Death moves quietly in the barn.
There is the stream
that runs under
& black trees stirred to the roots
by the stove-cold air. I
would only stay long enough
to fill my pot. Long enough to see
the white wool rise with the rain.

The earthworm jar

The basement door opens
& earth spills out,
fat blood-red earthworms
running like skinned snakes
out of a garbage hamper.
We live over their house.

How did they get there?
Old man by the mailbox heap
finds a ball of them
glistening in dew
& thinks, who passes through
a worm could be a chief
or sage,
& puts them in a pocket.

They are almost lunch
to a frying pan
until grandfather
takes them to their jar.
He covers them with leftovers
fit for a king.
How else to feed who wait
underneath for our meal?

When I go down
the soft, spongy stairs,
blood rushes in my ears.
My job is to bring the slops.
It is dark,
the way just before being

rescued from a dream
where my mouth
is stuffed with earth.

When I go down,
I think I hear
lemon peels dissolving
in their bodies.
I think I hear
how a heart
lives in a jar.

Absence of light

Who scrapes the other side
of the road, do you hear
the rope dragging
another body from the brush
to the initials
carved from the tar?

In dark, not even stars
are safe as the red
embers travel like eyes
on the wall's other side,
like hungry eyes
wanting to bring blood to
the scrawled name.

Opossum, I reach across
to touch your hair
& the dark heat clinging to
your back like a brand.
It is night
when spiders click &
& hair roots of corn
shiver & silks probe
dead air for life.
There is another word
for trying to see
what we are. Listen.
Not where light falls
on the animal soul.
A beer can & the long metal
arm throwing it
from the mountain top

& the men cramped in
their company caps.

There is another word
for the dark,
in letters through which
fire flickers. Listen.

Gallows day

The sky is falling, white shreds of skin,
soft hands on my back, feeling for
winter bruises. My father's hand
laid on me these long dead years.

It is the aspens that crave the long
dark coat that puts on early dusk,
candles by the bedside altars, salt
meat & barley dreams. They want to see
who bends to the soup, hungry for
brocade curtains, the broom that sweeps
the floor into a corner of the heart
& forgets. They want the old stories
the rebbe tells of how the world sheds
its aches & turns young & reckless
on the pathways.

I heard of the old woman who knitted
a web. White whiskers of hanged men
stuck to it, circles within
circles. Light stayed in her house
all night.

It was a healing, burning old
bread in a white heap, just off the side
where pavement ends, so no one
is hurt. A blessing to the old wheat,
smoke rises thinly to the sky. Words
of the right order or trees
would singe with fire. Under the cloth
the bruise is such a warning. I ache
with the strain of plaiting straight

rows. Let the spider make
what song there is.

By noon, their legs dangle in the
devil-wind, long spent, & I have
swept my floor a dozen times,
trying to remember where it is
I come from.

Purpose of a cat

One daughter of night
the cat
calls from the cellar
window.
In my dream, I am
distracted, choosing
a path overgrown
with red fern.

The roads branch
the way the gold-tongued
frogs grow legs
from the moist earth.
One leads to
a high place
beyond the crossroads.
But in my ears,
cat scratches
like chalk on
a slate board.

It is love she wants,
to rub it against the frigid
grip of solitude.
To see, to feel,
is not enough,
She wants to crawl
under my skin.

Under my skin
at night, a cat prowls,
crawling red trees of lungs

down to where the swamp
builds liquids of life.
Under my skin,
she is silent.
She fishes by the quiet
old sea.

I walk in the night,
awake. Dark rays &
coelacanths
swim in the sea
of this man.
He catches what he can,
forms hauled up
from radiant waters.
Sea-creatures like dark
organs line the shore.

On the shore the cat sits,
at the window
to my ocean.
She waits for dawn.
At dawn she slits
the gullets open
& lets the man fall out.

When planes drop from the sky

At dusk, a new sun gleams,
a golden body
like an eagle's drops
over the edge
trailing silent white gauze,
& I am happy how
the hand fits inside the glove
& the bowstring doesn't hurt
when pulled ever tauter.
It is safe to aim
at the fuselage
moving quickly past my gaze
because the pilot commands
forbidden borders.
He is not worried
by gunners who see
in the dark.

But what drops the plane
just overhead?
Men scarcely look up
when the low rumble herds
into some distant canyon
to break the earth open
& stampede the worms.
Men have read how diplomats
leave the wind to spin
in its own tight circle
& drop fertile thoughts
to the ground.
They know how nerves
turn to steel

& give death a bad name.
They say, it's a good
day for flying.
 Never mind the rain
that blackens children's dolls
or the dead sea rising to
wash their feet.
It is the jet diving from
its perch in the clouds
I run from.
Crashing through bramble
after a sheltering tree
or a flap of tent.
It drops like a stone
tied to a rope, thrown overboard.
Down the rungs
of my spine
till it snaps.

I scatter like a crowd
near a bomb.
I know what my dreams tell,
how the kamikaze spin
rights itself when my breath
is gone,
& my body is a wreck
laying among the leaves.
The squirrels strangely
show no panic,
gathering seeds
under my nails.
Under, where I hide
my soul.

The blue sky is empty
as a rearview mirror
& a drone aches on
like a passing train,
like a pulse
in the sky's wrist.
Planes of all nations yield
to the night as men
in the cockpits watch
enemy lights.

My heart is radar,
four chambers,
two right, two left.
The blip where the truth
is
hides, circling round
my face.
My face I hide
like a child
who shot at the sun
& hit it.

Stacking the woodpile by moonlight

Cracks of light
men build high by moon,
a ladder to the cold stars,
their hands
bleeding to build
higher,
& how wood chucked on top
opens more cracks, &
how they joke about
cutting their skin,
hungry for their blood.

Through the stove door,
I see them chasing the boys away.
They dance in & out
of moonlight, bobbing,
swaying under the logs.
Dancing in their arms
they hold--a moon.
There is no one else.
Old woman breath of fire
fogs the windows,
& the river melts
pulling children under
like frozen trees,
like stick-dolls
under the bridge.

There is an animal who lives
in the cracks. In my dreams,
a dog I incite to dive
under ice & bring back
the ones Inushka took away.

Inushka, silver-haired woman
of winter.
It scurries away as I
whisper, We are all one.
Now it is weasel
now eel, slithering along
the ice, now waves
spreading a sand blanket
over boys
in Inushka's bed.

As it snows
log after log
warms us & melts
the blood-ice men haul in.
There is the moon trapped
in the gravel bank.
It is no time for light
to climb the roof
& pretend the snow
to be stars.
I listen for the heavy breath,
for the hooting & howling,
for the boys
to knock snow
from their boots.
In the room,
the air sharp with cinnamon
& a log whining
for its mother.
In the dark, you can hear
them playing,
the smooth sound of rocks
tumbling,
tumbled in the waterfall.

Resurrection

Who comes to drink
at the rabbit pool
is no longer animal,
but a big, brown spot
where the tire tread
cut night softly
in two.

There were brakes
shrieking in pain,
& then boys were trading
the skin
for matches
& safety pins.
With a half flick
of a knife,
they start a rabbit
fire.

The taxidermist is
clumsy.
He plunges in at the gut
& rabbit lives again.
I cannot look
at how the flesh throbs
with the heat
of death.
I cannot find the word
to stop it.

Around the pit,
the boys clamor for
the prize.

Long & stringy,
it is a part
meaning something
only to the animal.
Pulling it out
jerks the rabbit
back to life
again.

When I look up,
the men are coming
with thick rope
to pry
flattened bones
from the tar.
There is the secret
mark
left on their boots.
Gasoline won't
erase it.

It is there
at dawn
all caution &
good sense, saying
enough to outsmart death.
But it is different
at dusk, I know.
At dusk, it is a slick
meaning mischief.
At dust, it is the body
waiting to live
another life.

Feast Days & Glory

Making turtle soup

This day has a shell
thick & gray as it lumbers
crossing under the hedges.
There is a brute brain
& nothing more.
A beak snaps
at the orange sun
worming through the grass.

Old woman sharpens
her knife from the glove
compartment. No thing
strengthens a sagging body
like the turkle soup.
Though big as her,
with the tail, she plops
the creature
on the plates of its hump.
Sun comes back out.

Iron claw for one hand,
she calls her daughter.
Its armor has no head
unless you pull one out.
It takes two of them &
all their strength
to get that day out
& when it come
she chop it off.
That is the end to sadness.
Blink. It gone.
Black turtle bloodruns from the sun
down the highway & into the jaw

still snapping
the knife in two.
It is the heart they want.
Grandmother takes an oar &
stirs the life back in.
It beats in her hand.
Twahk, twahk.
Smell from the pot
tells the story of
April mud to her veins.
She rocks & listens.

Soup is rich & steamy
with chunks of meat
swimming its pond-green scum.
Young man sun sits down.
She takes a shine to him.
Tells about the door
above her bedroom.
That man just eat & eat,
warming the earth.
Come night, he take
her away with him.
On the roadside, dog-flower
& pigweed line up
for the entrails.

Labyrinth

One gosling meets another
from under water as sun
reddens its tail at
the pond's mouth.

They dive for roots
& one comes up trailing a cord
to the dark center.
The innards twitch
as their bills unwind
the skein water has wound
since before there was time.

It is a great medicine
they all chase without
a mind to who's caught. Fifteen
geese being caged by greed
& the ruckus of fifteen more
below.

I can see how the succulent
vine pulls, coming
from so far down. The geese
are sinking. I want to
warn them. I can see
the red fox sinking
into the red rim
of the pond.

They will all meet
in a place
of great passion,

food set for body
& spirit, where
host & guest join
in one feast.

Herring run

The stream fed by black alder
built walls of stone
we cross to pick
mint for tea. Tea
beneath the morning candle
burnt low by the men
fishing the night moon,
leaving a pale shell
in the dawn sky west.
Snail shells to count what
is to be gathered.

Hot jugs & baskets
of rolls. I help pack
for the alewife that run
the moon tide, turning
back to the brooks
of ancestors. Tea
that boils along the sand,
leaving us shells
as the boats are eaten.
The women in long skirts
sweep us into stone
alleys to keep us from
the wind.

I wait, mending
nets, count
if the sea, once too heavy,
kept a man from turning.
How the keel
makes a brook that draws

water falling easily
from the bow into
the waiting lips of the
lobster pot.
Mint to keep the bilge
down when the skein
is torn & the sea
swallows the wall whole.

Stitch flower beside
yellow rattle whose dry
shells call *sheeh, sheeh*
to the wind. I walk
softly on the moon
made pale by our fires.
The air is mint,
even salt
is chased back
under our skin.
Streams of fish swim
under black alder
back to the heart pool.
The way I lie
on my stomach, counting
out waves.

The importance of getting home

The nerves unwind
a few snarls
& the glaring night
that does not burn a hole
through my retina
comes in another way,
from under the pools of eyelids
that clear the road
of scares,
& I
begin to understand
all those travel poems.

Travel poems of coffee
stops & green smoke
& the press of metal
under the tongue.
The way we get out
& stretch
a muscle that cramps
inside the chest.
Who we are, foot on
the petal
after all these hours.

The bodies woven
in optical fibers
of headlights
are broken glances
of inside the windshield.
They are the ones we pray

to, praying for a wind home.
Listen to the wheel.
The ones who leapt
into the dark curve
of a reflected face
did not.
They are the speed limit.

We are all those ones
not stopped for--
mother, father, husband,
wife--because we could not,
listening for a sound we knew,
a clink of the teapot
against an opal ring.
It is what we lean into,
over the miles,
leaning over the kitchen
table trying to follow
words, slow & dreamy,
we ourselves say
of one long tough
ride home.

Setting the table

The winter sun is putting us
back to sleep
in the kitchen window.
Soup is sweating roses
on the wallpaper
sprouting from brown mildew.
I don't think we'll
ever have to eat again.

In the winter, I say,
my heart is fasting.
Like a squirrel's tail
I found today by itself
then a rabbit's,
nothing's connected.

In the winter, I say,
there's nothing I crave.
The vine is long &
withered &
sap moves
like guests leaving
after the meal.

But in winter,
I have secret powers.
A few spare words
& a stove valve hisses.
Ice melts
like a beating heart.
At midnight,
my ears flatten

back like a cat's.
Underground, seeds pop
their pods
like frozen soda bottles.
I hear them sprout
wiry green hair.
Underground in winter
I know dark rivers,
run through dreamers'
mouths
into rusted cauldrons
that soon bush
with spring flowers.
I know the tide
does not stop.

Come spring, when sap
runs the riot act,
we choke on sulfur &
molasses that gurgles
on the kitchen stove.
My eyelids are heavy
racing about looking
for love.
I don't want to eat.
I am hungry again
for basement rock.
I want what bodies
knew
before their appetite
boils for blood.

Necklace of fox teeth

In a fox-grin,
pale shell moon finds
an old corset
on the junk heap.
It is loose from wearing
too many fat years.
She slyly puts it on.

Now she is beautiful.
She climbs the reeds,
humming dawn in.
She is a slim-
waisted wasp
on the fox-tail down.
When a wind comes up,
she is a whalebone
made of dead sailors.

She sings fifteen men
on a dead man's chest.
I find the collar
& whittle
a scrimshaw hook.
Butter it with bacon
& leave it flaming
where fox fire burns.

Spyglass moon looks down
& sees where the fox
blood leads.
Up around the crown

& down the hill,
fox is on the trail of
fox.

As the river gets
wider at the mouth,
fox is closing
in on the red sea.
I will not look at
how the blood
slinks along behind,
aching for the scent
of life.

Head of mother moon
flung up
in the trees
watches fox
watch fox.
Fox is after
what eats at him.
He snuffs for the whale.
Each breath
a drop closer
to the belly
of the beast.

At sunset,
I see the spume
redden
the pond.
Fox-smell is on

my tongue.
Wake of a hundred moons
swims out to the center
where the light
falls in.
From the shriveled
carcass, I take
the mangy coat
& put it over
my head.
His jaw relaxes &
smiles up at the moon.
The reeds sing
fifteen men on a
dead man's chest.

All night, I walk
circles round
the pond, leading
the fox-moon on.
She walks away from
the blood following me.
My tail is
the night wind
flicking the reeds
ffft, ffft.

The bride's remedy

What grows, dandelion & mustard
green, around the kiln
has no idea of fire.
Succulent stalk, you dance with
young girls under the yellow sun
dreaming your dowry of beds.

Inches away behind a brick
compound under a steel grate,
the sun does more than cause red
blemishes. Earth is smelted
under an iron will. Made
to obey the hand, to seal
that grip & pour rivers
on the parched fields.

The bitter herbs that grow
in my garden bed.
They wilt when the sun objects
to green skin & wants roots
to pierce earth's molten core.
The old Syrian women
comes each spring to pluck them
& place them on broken crockery
for her daughter's health.
Dandelion for a fever.
Mustard keeps the waters clean.

Her song is a river
of fennel root. Root white
sun, hot to the tongue.
She chews on nerve, spits

green fountains, & up
spring stalks bubbling
from the kiln top. Whole cities
dance like houris in their serenade.

Only by night when dandelion wine
has cured the sun's head &
earth sleeps under a dew,
I want to stop a moment
& tell her about the fire,
I want to say it is hot, &
no matter what you dream
all will be forgiven.

Harvest song

This is the month of shag
bark & warm nights.
Silk melts over ears
of standing corn. The month
katydids listen at midnight
for the ice knife
that severs life,
that makes the stalks
whisper *shush, shu*.

As we swing, my son & I
shucking corn, stripping
threads of life
from white knuckles
while the leaves grow
higher at our feet.
What we grip falls
scuffing like dry leaves.
Unsaid things falling
like dead leaves.

In far off fields,
where we filled our bag,
the rustle of women's
skirts & a heavy perfume
as in nights home alone.
It is where her dusk
finds mice gleaning
for kernels of yellow
moon, before being a bloodspot
under a fox's maw.

Now it is quiet,
we hear only bark
springing from the trunk.
Not corn squealing
wrenched from its silk
or flesh wrenched squealing
from its spine
by black of night.
Just our throats
dry from holding on,
sheehing as words are torn
from the chest
before the long freeze
of winter sets in.

The Quarry

Migration

Three geese
make a family
in blind confusion,
gleaning,
& the yellow corn
scatters yellow suns
from so many hungry bills.
It is warming
cold earth clotted
under their webbed feet.

The geese are fat.
They crane
their necks into green
air, to swallow
that light too.

Grandmother grabs one
from the coldbox
stretching its neck
to old city sun.
The skin
is the soft, plucked skin
of her elbows.
It has a sheen like corn
after she pulls
the silk from the ear
before dropping it
into the pot.

She mixes poppyseed
& goosefat

while we are lighting
the yarzeit
for the son she had,
shot down in flight.
It gutters
like a prayer.
I hear the sound
of stubble wings
against a glass sky.

The kitchen is full
of grandmother's
scaldings.
It is time for harvest
& death.
War is almost over.
Stovefire repeats
the song
that geese sang
last night picking
at mice entrails
left from a fox feast.
That is the way of
fire.

There is hunger
all around the table
but I cannot eat
the cake.
The mirrors are
draped in black.
At night on my down

pillow, sleep runs
away
wanting to bury me
in its soft feathers.
From my watch
in a strange room,
I hear
geese hissing a mile up.
They slip slowly
south, toward
a land that never dies,
to forage for dreams
& prayers.
I listen,
my blood frozen.

I listen to
how the air between us
hisses as they fly,
how like corn stubble
I am
rooted,
mute in place.

Raking leaves in spring

I am thinking of work
done out of season.
How much harder it is
when leaves
have wintered &
cling with longing
to earth.
The tide is
involved.

From under leaves,
the motherwort
shoots its blossom up,
from under those deaths
that nourish.
Its shaft
that comes to my hand
without tugging.

In the hospital lot
that late spring
it grew rank.
I tore you
a sprig
to keep
behind the locked doors.
It was already something
old in your palm.

They had cut your
hair short.
You could do

no raking.
White scentless flowers
were as close
to earth
as you came.

Green roots
& no strength
to keep you from
ripping the garden up.
We all--
mothers, fathers,
sisters, brothers--
held on.
It was against
the tide.
You left one day
while leaves were
heavy & wet &
out of season.
Once exposed,
millipedes dodged
the young warrior sun.
You left early &
I tell myself
the hard work
of parting
is never done.

Surrender

Stone grinding
on stone.
I love
the gunpowder
smell
& how biceps pop
prying rocks
from their socket.

But come evening
I see
dark
topple the wall
tier by tier,
& my old man arms
cannot
stop stone
dropping into
cold, dead
earth.

Day Laborers

Like orange peels
sprawling from a lunchbag,
newts scatter
the migrant bus's wake
along the backwater road.
October sun is still warm
enough to keep them
from stiffening
into pretty sumac leaves
for the highway crew.

On their backs
they stride after the workers,
swimming in exhaust
from the antique motor.
They are there, busy
when it parts.
Unlike the migrants,
they are in no hurry
to cross dry land
& weather is no concern.
They are a tribe
without a hunting ground,
laborers without a job.

The tired ones look
through lidless eyes
bellyside up at me,
inverted, transplanted.
They cannot stop staring
at me between cars passing them
wrongway up

while the shadows mount.
It is confusing them
that I stay.

Once in a while, one moves
its legs in slow motion
& stops.
Its soft belly is
unprotected
like my boy's fall
just before sleep.
Under the white collar,
a life throbs
the way a leaf trickles down
the throat of the wind.

There are the dreams
that keep the workers
from falling off ladders.
The trees are closing
in on us all.
I can't help kneeling
touching a finger
on the pulse.

The hunters: 30 years after

Men in orange suits
walk through orchards
wearing orange leaves.
It is before dawn,
when the wind is heavy
with deer-breath.
Nothing wants to move
from its dream.

The sun is orange too.
It is just up, shining on
the day a president
is killed.
It sets fire to guns
& pampas grass.
Grandfather sun is up
& an orange dust
falls on the dew.

In the scaffold of light,
I am stalking the hunters,
building shadows
of guns
in my empty hands.
In my hands,
a nation waits with prayers.
I want to squeeze
the trigger & change
everything.

Blood asks
the way a river asks,

& when it floods the earth,
our lies burn in its heat,
in fear's heat.
It asks the impossible.
It asks we remember
& wait.

The assassin
goes scot-free.
In the paper we find
he has a full belly.
His truth is simple greed.
He is dead
before his words find
light.

The light falls
where it will.
We say, where it falls
will suffice.
When we are true,
we know the bullet
fits the barrel &
another has been cut down
because he stood
in the way.

We are all passing through
one another,
hunger and hunted,
stalking what stalks us.
Dawn is an air raid.

I see leaves dropping
slowly where the body falls.
The air rings in silence.
The men, who are foreigners,
are gone.

I have forgotten
how to make the war-cry.
It is not death
that wakens me
but the ping of a pebble
thrown sharply against glass.

High tension

Old squirrel pops off
The electric
Making the page dark,
Darker than the ink
That wires spurt
When our lamps cut off.

A detonation
That sets me diving
To my hole for a candle
& match. In the dark
words never mean the same
as in the sun. In the dark,
wire grows barbed and razor
& blood doesn't hide.

In one invisible flash,
Squirrel dies a sky death,
Falls rigid as a sumac stick
Beside the phone pole.
Dogs run off, grey fur
In their mouths, dark eyes,
New words barred in their teeth.

There is the hum
Of new power
In the quiet of death.
Cold dark light of an outage.
A man gets out of the
Yellow truck with a fuse.
Twin eyes of his search light
Hold the box steady

To plug the new one in.
Look back
At the house lamp &
The hum is gone.

When I go back & listen to
The blank pages, my hand
Twitches like a squirrel tail.
My hand is drawn to power,
Remembers how to unscrew
The bulb, the feel of the magnet
In the socket, the jerk
When the current discovers you.
It knows what squirrels
Do on black nights
When they are tired
Of the news.

Son of my Loins,
Son of my Blood

Returning to the nest

The young copperhead
is all alone.
It is a river running
back to its nest,
a brown headband
that knows the inside
of everything.
With gasoline, the men
blow it to high heaven.

I am alone,
the world runs through me,
charred pit for a mouth.
My words keep secrets
from running home.

All lives I have lived
live still,
in a nest of ribbons.
They lie over each other,
sisters & brothers
of one house,
quarrelsome & loving.
They weave
no finished plait.

In one life,
there is a boy
left out in a game of hiding.
They must find the nest
& join it,
not telling the secret.

The sun is cold
& reptilian
running home to the stars.
Once there were many boys.
Now he is last.
Running alone.

The last life
runs home through me
with its secret powers.
It skitters frantic
to escape
the final conflagration.
Its love is feared.
I say prayers
for the youngest.
I do not say where
the nest is
or who will find him there.

Boy sleeping

Under jaw-red hair,
your one crocodile eye
never sleeps while
the other is drooping
below the mud
waiting for dark prey.
It cannot see.

Under my hood
I am keeping watch over
your reptilian form
like the little bird
on your brow.
I am quicker
than your good eye
since I race it for
the blood & escape
unscathed.

We eat of one
meal
& breathe
the same air,
yet all the others
are lifeless stone
under your look.

There was the time
the razor-thin ridge
of your back
lay in wait
for my neck to soften.

But I have learned
to love
warily, unafraid.
When I return
to myself,
your jaws unclench
even as the tongue
hisses fire,
& we are again
so close we become
seer &
soul.

Medusa's head
was one-eyed,
the other eye blinded
by grief.
By what patience?
One anger numbing
another
until the whole world
is silent stone.

Crystalwalking

Light glinting from the surface
the sun rolls back &
outside & in your eyes
faults show, sharp edges,
true corners of the gray road.

Nothing glowers this noon
of winter except frost roots
of a Coke bottle, a city
exploded on asphalt
dreams of lithrum,
rushing home to lunch.

We have no purpose than to walk
squinting sideways, my son.
Walk the blue bowl of sky
where it rims our feet,
go forth. Find where quartz
meets the dazzling world.
I want your strength
to feel the air divide
for you, wrapping itself around
your back like an eagle's claw.
Those you meet like this are
also true.

Through clouds of breath, light
leaping from the stream & back,
then lost to the next rapids.
Animals suck the breath from
inside where our fathers would
wait patiently, reach behind

themselves the way a bear does
poaching salmon. Pulling the blade in,
walking it, kneeling
at its source. To hunt what
sets itself in the blood-reach
of our veins.

What we take is earned
drop by drop.
Each step, in dark or light,
counting as stars do
without a total but exact.
Otherwise the stone
melts in the palm
overheated like a late spawn
lost overnight in a pocket.

If we do not find, the world
keeps count, glints
from its only sun. Do not know
when. My frozen fingers
broken skin in pure winter light,
your breath close to my ear
sparks in the river between us
& leaps across, crystal drum
beating the cave of your hand.

Rosebush

This is war,
the bush stripped bare
for winter.
Thorns glisten
with razor-sharp ice.
In the heart of it,
a wren's nest,
deserted & alone.

This is the bush
that teaches us war.
Its long white spines
are a lace
that lets go
our broken vows
& drops them shattered
on the infertile ground.

A man goes to this bush
& feels his skin
stretched tight
in its shadow.
His bones are crushed
by the angry hammers
of his heart.
This is what I give to my son.
The silent space
surrounding each blade
of light.

The bush is heavy
with its dead.

A deer licks a branch
for thirst.
A mouse gnaws its spine.
A bird reconnoiters.
I show this also to my son,
that we are men,
a thousand miles of desert
bow to the need to cross
over our own skin.
The rose red sun shines from
our face & the green grass
grows under our boots.

Cardboard wings

Seven years cram
An empty bag
With famine.
It comes each night
To starve you of sleep.
At the seventh star,
Soft fingers untie
The noose
& let go a feather.
It drops where
Imagination feeds
The hungry ghosts.
Your dream-catcher is full.

On the carpet,
The blue bird of fear
Makes a nest
Of corrugated paper.
It will hatch a flickering fire.
It broods as
Stars torn from its beak fall.
The empty sockets
Fill up with bones.

Seeds of water fall.
They burn our skin
With tongues like lizards.
Listen. It is the speaking
Our fathers knew
Placing their hands
On things
Raw, glistening, young.

On our palms,
Their love is etched.

As you climb, my son,
The acid rain
Sears the smooth body
Of earth, eating through pods.
Already, green vines reach above
Ready for you in their soft arms,
In the curling tendrils
That keep safe
Words spoken in the sun.

How to shoot a crow

His head rests in the crook
of my arm, my son
who dreams of the tent flap
open, men talking unseen
around a cold fire.
My son who knows
tomorrow in the crook of his arm.
The sky draws back the bow
he will lift
& lets fly the feathers
through his nerves.
In sleep, the heart pounds
under the breastplate
of his tribe, ours.

Does it matter
an old crows flies,
squawking hoarsely from
breakfast by the cornfield?
Old yellow sun
squints because a grain of sand
catches in his eye.
Suddenly it threatens rain.
Roots that hold us
each to our place
loosen. They open
their mouths to drink.

The notch that loves
feeling the string.
How we are all notched,
walking this earth,

ready to be drawn
by a crooked arm
of the woman or man we are
to be. Crow flies
above our mouths, having fed
on the soil of our life.
That is why the bow
sings. That is why
the boy draws back.

My son, your arm flexes
like wind across the drawn string.
Black feathers brush
your cheek. Whose heat
melts the wax fear?
Whose blood bleeds on
the yarrow sticks?
Before you look up,
your eye already swallowed his.
Before you shoot, your arrow
already caught his beak.

On a Bridge of Shells

Tutilltown Bridge

Men wear hard hats
so the years won't hit them,
peeling girders back
that used to be a bridge.
Sawed-off bolts
like old shell casings
in their pockets
jangle & gather rust.
There is music as they cut,
music that keeps the doves away.

Now, another deadend road
in a county full of
shanty bars & hard talk,
though much is left undone.
On the barreltops the men stacked,
yellowjackets dance confusedly.
They stumble & fall
like drunken soldiers.
The frost has made them
high with death.
Though the air is calm,
their flight is
bewildered. So many
drop silent to the ground.

They are a lost tribe.
In its steel belly,
the bridge once held their nest.
Now they camp on apple
cores & empty Coke cans
until dusk comes again.

Sometimes I see
columns of them dart
in disbelief midway across
the river. It is a
last foray. They are almost
a strand to the other side.
Over the churning water,
they are almost a bridge.

I want to tell them everything
depends on speed.
I want to say how crossings
are always chancy
unless you have a home.

Bullfrog's horn

Rain came last night &
washed the creek away.
Not a drop left.
Old bullfrog
who kept us lying
flesh on flesh--
he's on the roadside, dead.

Who else will keep us
awake, counting night
traffic to drown
the salty groans?
That old goat,
why'd he stop croaking?

Upside down spots
like an iris,
like when we stare
at the morning sun &
look away. Mouth
yellow as swallowing
the sun.

He's already dry when the flies
come up a day late,
& skin peeling back
like cigarette paper.
Who are we to stop to look?
Headlights behind
are brown suns in the fog,
like the sharp words we blurred
by looking rearview,

& the dumb retreats
when the jaw locked
with us inside,
& the salt in morning tea
after dreams of swimming
in the backseat.

There is a gap
where the mouth was,
a line where the earth fits
like a red spot
on a caved-in yolk.
Let's go in & swallow
the hunger of this night.
Let's go & toss
the bones aside &
see where we can lie
underneath.

Wash day

What a dust!
Pound a nail in to keep
the ground together.
The men march
singing a song of politics.
There's hardly any time
to find a stone.

The dust is getting on
the clothes I just hung,
& they want to hang a man
who knows. He'll swing
from a tree
& tell the truth.
How their words
change things from live
to dead. By the roadside,
dust shrivels the ivy.
I think they are afraid.

What's there to fear
from a song like mine?
The laundry won't get dirty.
No need to pound a hammer.
Old boy, when you dance,
dust sticks to your soles.
If there's a sad note,
it doesn't hang in air
like a sharp hook
so that men want
dangle their words &
cut out others' tongues.

The roads are all covered
like my wash.
No place to go & nothing
to wear. Even the rifles
have throats clogged
with the stuff.
Time to unload & start over.
Maybe the dust will keep
everything nailed down.
Maybe the men will stay home.

Dance at the rim

The ladder tossed & dropped.
Swarms of boys are out to climb it,
one has a turtle captive
between the rungs to hold
the world up with.

Yellow sun fading gleams more
on that tortoise shell
than all the aluminum bars.
It makes me want to sing.

For the shouting, you can't hear
the soft plop as shell
gives in. When the car drives
the dim road by the marsh, you
know a second later. No need
to go back & check. In blood tracks,
turtle walks away from its death.

Soft moon & moss
unearths caves & notches to hook
fingers onto. Where turtle
flesh rubbed, worn bone
chipped at the edges.
Base of a mound.

I collect ladder &
pieces of shell, thinking
this is the way
to get to the bottom.
Where a body
can dance without slipping through
the rungs.

Spring salamander

A thousand new eyes
a lizard born
clawing at the cliff
tearing scruff pine
an ear of thunder against.

Thunder is a word
I feel in the damp
house, snatching at
a tail of things
that darts anxiously out
of sight. Thunder
that broke the earth open
& let the creature
out.

Things that run
from my grasp,
a trail of
pine needles
to silent underground
streams. From there
to mix the graves
of my tribe
with unborn ones,
hatched from stone
shells, & to shake
our sleeping bones
when we walk
along unknown paths.
Who walks them is
a brother.

All day, I pick
broken shells from
my floor, set them
new eyes
on the pine hearth.

They watch who
walks behind my eyelids
& crawls the precipice
of my chest.
They hear trees
crash thunderously
at the bottom
near where the path
begins.

The backstop is a tree

A nest behind the sign
sparrows dart from, unread letters.
Men duck, not to let
the words hit them in the face
like a missed pitch.
Fledglings try the air
for themselves, so many
flying objects swooping
among the men playing ball.

What do the letters say?
The sign's too high for reading
& even if you wanted to
it's streaked from the weather
& the slop of nesting.

I stop to watch
the new pitcher & end watching
the young ones pushed out
before knowing the rules
of the game. So many
floaters & knucklers.
Pitcher can't catch
the signals the catcher gives
so he ends by throwing
the rosin bag at them.

It raises a big white dust.
The world is white &
there is no nest or men
only a tornado of coughs
with hawking of dry throats

& a great confusion about the
direction of the sun.
The sparrows seemed to have
escaped, camping out on a
nearby bleacher. I throw
crumbs to celebrate.
The whiteout somehow lets
missing words shine
like neon for all the world
to read, & you can't help
reading them. No Spitting.

Roadblock

It is time that moves
rotten boards piled up
across a road. A
barrio none of us
can cross.
Two small
boys run from under a
tin roof that keeps
the sun from falling
in.
Chased by the old man
whose car is
blocked.

His horn fills
my ears. Wild geese
chasing nothing
I ever dream of.
They do not let up
though there is no
avoiding the job.

The boys are in
a dark woods.
Bramble scratches
open their legs,
But they don't stop.
It is memory that catches
them after the run.
Scissors of a woman
who is always
gathering grapeleaves.

Pile reaches higher
than the blood.
Old man can barely
walk the lowest board.
Who will pick that house
up again, dragged
back to life
from where roots ate it?
Who will find
the way home again?

A woman who always is
gathering grapeleaves.

Typeset in ITC Garamond, a re-cutting of the classic face designed by Claude Garamond (Garamont) in c.1531. He was one of the first punch cutters to work independently of printers; perfected designs of roman type and introduced it to replace the Gothic then commonly used.

Illustrations are by the renowned and highly respected English illustrator and wood engraver Thomas Bewick, (1753-1828). The illustrations used here were engraved principally as tail-pieces for his *General History of Quadrupeds & History of British Birds*. Originally published as a group in 1827 as *Vignettes*.

Designed and typeset by Martin Moskof.